INSIDE THE NHL

Washington Capitals

Ramey Temple

AV2 BY WEIGL
MEDIA ENHANCED BOOKS
ADDED VALUE • AUDIO VISUAL

www.av2books.com

AV² provides enriched content that supplements and complements this book. Weigl's AV² books strive to create inspired learning and engage young minds in a total learning experience.

Your AV² Media Enhanced books come alive with...

Audio
Listen to sections of the book read aloud.

Key Words
Study vocabulary, and complete a matching word activity.

Go to **www.av2books.com**, and enter this book's unique code.

Video
Watch informative video clips.

Quizzes
Test your knowledge.

BOOK CODE

Q425539

Embedded Weblinks
Gain additional information for research.

Slide Show
View images and captions, and prepare a presentation.

AV² by Weigl brings you media enhanced books that support active learning.

Try This!
Complete activities and hands-on experiments.

... and much, much more!

Published by AV² by Weigl
350 5th Avenue, 59th Floor
New York, NY 10118
Websites: www.av2books.com   www.weigl.com

Library of Congress Control Number: 2014951922

ISBN 978-1-4896-3194-7 (hardcover)
ISBN 978-1-4896-3195-4 (single-user eBook)
ISBN 978-1-4896-3196-1 (multi-user eBook)

Printed in the United States of America in Brainerd, Minnesota
1 2 3 4 5 6 7 8 9 0   19 18 17 16 15

032015
WEP050315

Senior Editor Heather Kissock
Art Director Terry Paulhus

Photo Credits
Every reasonable effort has been made to trace ownership and to obtain permission to reprint copyright material. The publishers would be pleased to have any errors or omissions brought to their attention so that they may be corrected in subsequent printings.

Weigl acknowledges Getty Images and iStock as its primary image suppliers for this title.

Washington Capitals

CONTENTS

Introduction

The Washington Capitals began as an **expansion franchise** in 1974. Owner Abe Pollin won the bid for the team and promised to build an arena in the District of Columbia suburb of Landover, Maryland. The Capital Centre became the new home of the Capitals as well as the Washington Bullets, the National Basketball Association team that Pollin also owned. The fans got behind the team right away, despite the Capitals winning just eight games and suffering through the worst inaugural season in NHL history. The next few years were not much better.

Early in the 2014–2015 season, Alexander Ovechkin passed Peter Bondra to become the Capitals' all-time points leader.

Although the Caps would not make their first **playoff** appearance until 1983, they would soon become postseason regulars, qualifying for the playoffs every season from 1983 through 1996. The greatest season in Capitals history took place in 1998, when Olaf Kolzig, known as "Olie the Goalie," led the team to the Stanley Cup Final. They lost that series to the Detroit Red Wings in four games.

Nicklas Backstrom has played all of his seven NHL seasons with the Washington Capitals.

Washington CAPITALS

Arena Verizon Center

Division Metropolitan

Head Coach Barry Trotz

Location Washington, D.C.

NHL Stanley Cup Titles None

Nicknames Caps, Eagles

24
Playoff Appearances

2
Conference Finals

8
Division Championships

5
Hall of Famers

History

The Capitals have had
12
captains in team history.

Alex Ovechkin, the greatest player in team history, is not afraid to shoot from anywhere on the ice.

When the Capitals first began playing at the Capital Centre in 1974, the new arena was a bigger spectacle than the team itself. Due to competition from the **World Hockey Association (WHA)**, a league taking talent from the NHL at that time, the Capitals struggled to succeed. The story was much the same for the next few seasons, until they finally broke through in 1983 with their first playoff appearance.

In 1997, the team moved to the Verizon Center in Washington, D.C., a fitting location for the franchise, considering that D.C. had been awarded the team in the first place. A year later, the Capitals' best chance at a championship quickly disappeared when they faced a loaded Red Wings team in the 1998 Stanley Cup Final.

Today, the Capitals continue to field talented and competitive teams, headlined by their star left winger, Alexander Ovechkin. The Russian star quickly established himself during his 2005-2006 **rookie** season when he scored 106 points. A three-time Hart Memorial Trophy winner for Most Valuable Player (MVP), Ovechkin has not slowed down since and is a key part of the Capitals past, present, and future.

The Capitals lost all four games they played against the Red Wings in the 1998 Final.

The Arena

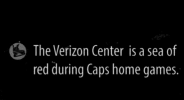

The Verizon Center is a sea of red during Caps home games.

The Capitals' current arena, the Verizon Center, first opened its doors on December 2, 1997. At that time, it was known as the MCI Center. The team had moved from its previous home at the Capital Centre in Landover, Maryland. Residents of the District of Columbia were ecstatic about this change. The arena, located in the bustling Seventh Street Corridor, got a brand new name in 2006, the Verizon Center. On December 2, 2007, the arena celebrated its 10th anniversary by installing the first ever true, indoor, high-definition LED scoreboard.

The Verizon Center is home to the Capitals, the Washington Wizards (NBA), Washington Mystics (WNBA), and the Georgetown Hoyas (NCAA). Music legends such as U2 and Barbara Streisand have performed at the Verizon Center as well. The arena is a cultural center and has been an important contributor to the city's revitalization. There are many restaurants in the arena in addition to a variety of concessions, specializing in everything from crab cakes to deli sandwiches.

The Verizon Center hosts an average of 220 events per year, including concerts featuring stars such as Usher.

Where They Play

British Columbia

Alberta

4

7

3

CANADA

Saskatchewan

Manitoba

14

Ontario

Washington

Montana

North Dakota

Minnesota

11

Wisconsin

Oregon

Idaho

South Dakota

8

Wyoming

UNITED

Iowa

Illinois

6

Nevada

Utah

Colorado

9

Nebraska

STATES

Kansas

Missouri

13

California

5

Arizona

2

New Mexico

Oklahoma

Arkansas

1

Texas

10

Mississ

Louisiana

Pacific
Ocean

MEXICO

Gulf of
Mexico

WESTERN CONFERENCE

PACIFIC DIVISION		CENTRAL DIVISION	
1 Anaheim Ducks	5 Los Angeles Kings	8 Chicago Blackhawks	12 Nashville Predators
2 Arizona Coyotes	6 San Jose Sharks	9 Colorado Avalanche	13 St. Louis Blues
3 Calgary Flames	7 Vancouver Canucks	10 Dallas Stars	14 Winnipeg Jets
4 Edmonton Oilers		11 Minnesota Wild	

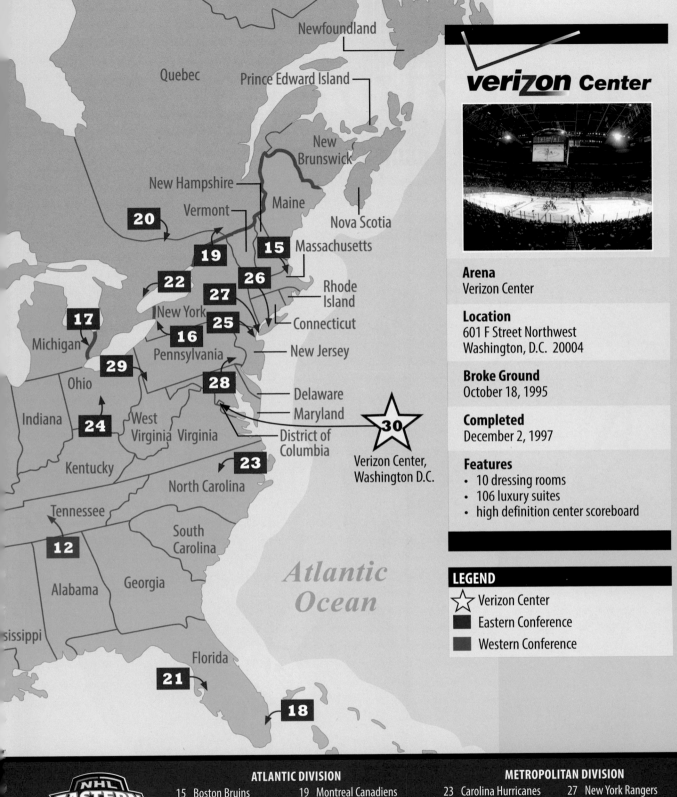

Newfoundland

Quebec

Prince Edward Island

New Brunswick

New Hampshire

Vermont

Maine

Nova Scotia

20

19

15 Massachusetts

22

26

Rhode Island

27

17

New York

25

Connecticut

Michigan

16

New Jersey

Pennsylvania

29

28

Ohio

Delaware

Indiana

Maryland

24

West Virginia   Virginia

District of Columbia

30

Kentucky

23

Verizon Center, Washington D.C.

North Carolina

Tennessee

South Carolina

12

Alabama

Georgia

Atlantic Ocean

ssissippi

Florida

21

18

verizon Center

Arena
Verizon Center

Location
601 F Street Northwest
Washington, D.C. 20004

Broke Ground
October 18, 1995

Completed
December 2, 1997

Features
- 10 dressing rooms
- 106 luxury suites
- high definition center scoreboard

LEGEND
☆ Verizon Center
■ Eastern Conference
■ Western Conference

NHL EASTERN CONFERENCE ★★★

ATLANTIC DIVISION

15	Boston Bruins	19	Montreal Canadiens
16	Buffalo Sabres	20	Ottawa Senators
17	Detroit Red Wings	21	Tampa Bay Lightning
18	Florida Panthers	22	Toronto Maple Leafs

METROPOLITAN DIVISION

23	Carolina Hurricanes	27	New York Rangers
24	Columbus Blue Jackets	28	Philadelphia Flyers
25	New Jersey Devils	29	Pittsburgh Penguins
26	New York Islanders	★ 30	Washington Capitals

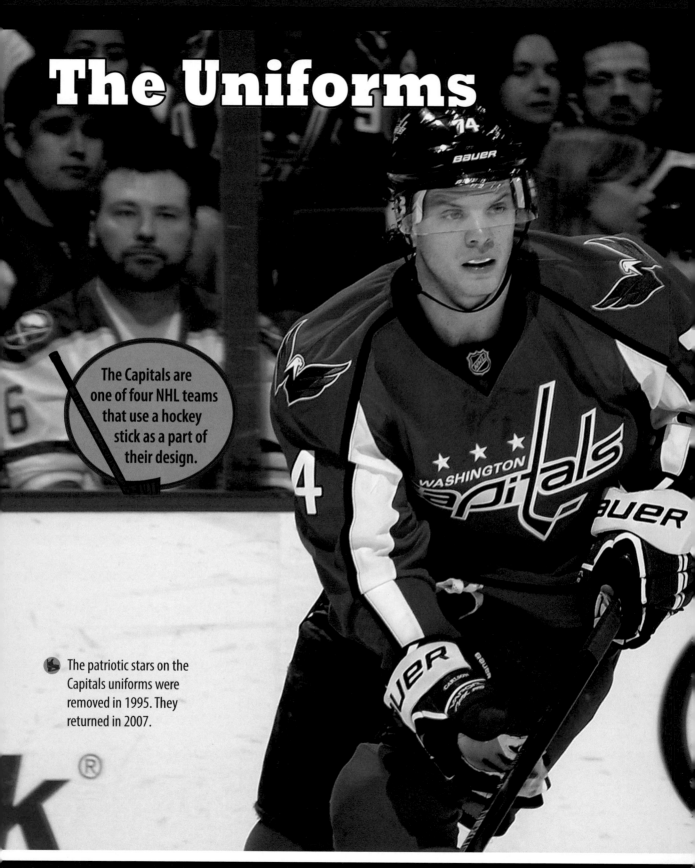

The Uniforms

The Capitals are one of four NHL teams that use a hockey stick as a part of their design.

The patriotic stars on the Capitals uniforms were removed in 1995. They returned in 2007.

The Capitals' colors are red, white, and blue, matching the American flag. In 1995, the uniform colors were changed to blue, black, and bronze. By 2007, the team decided to restore the original colors, to the delight of most long time fans.

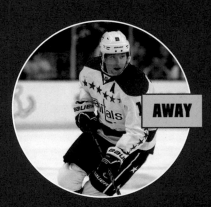

HOME

Today, the players wear red jerseys for home games and white jerseys on the road. On the front of the jersey, the word "Capitals" appears in a slanted font that has a hockey stick posing as the stem of the letter "T". The pants are blue for home games and red for away games. The red pants also boast stars along the side, adding to the Capitals' patriotic theme.

AWAY

Celebrating a goal in their home uniforms, in front of the D.C. fans, is always better than celebrating on the road.

Helmets and Face Masks

High-tech head gear protects the entire face and head, allowing goaltenders to make saves from their knees without risking serious **HEAD INJURIES**.

A rising star between the pipes, Braden Holtby has the size and athleticism to be the Caps starting goaltender for many years. His face mask is very patriotic, reminding some Caps fans of Vokoun's P.O.T.U.S. mask.

The Capitals players wear plain dark blue helmets for home games and white ones on the road. Goalies, on the other hand, can be more creative with the design of their helmets. Perhaps the best example is former Capitals goalie, Tomas Vokoun, who decorated his helmet with a very patriotic theme during the 2011–2012 season. Vokoun's famous mask is red, white, and blue with stars along the top of the helmet. It quickly became a fan favorite. There is a light blue bald eagle on both sides, and the helmet even has a name, P.O.T.U.S., which stands for "President of the United States." George Washington and Abraham Lincoln both appear on the mask, as well as a second bald eagle that appears on the chin area.

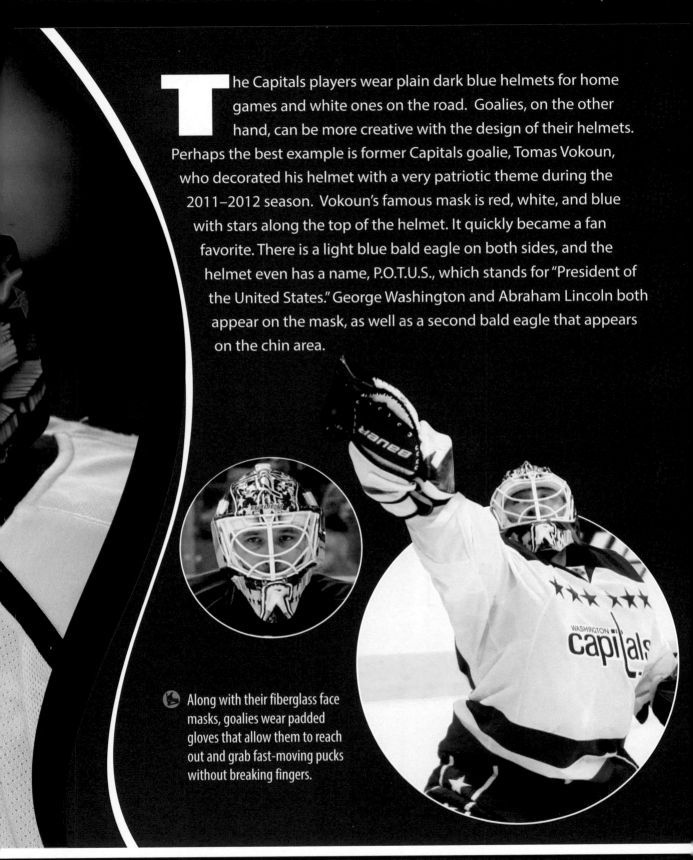

Along with their fiberglass face masks, goalies wear padded gloves that allow them to reach out and grab fast-moving pucks without breaking fingers.

The Coaches

 15 Barry Trotz coached the Nashville Predators for 15 seasons before he was hired to lead the Caps.

Barry Trotz tallied 557 wins in Nashville but never led the Predators past the conference semifinals.

The Capitals have had 17 coaches in their 40-year history. Their longest tenured coach is Bryan Murray, who led the Caps for nine seasons. The team has managed to qualify for the playoffs in 24 of the past 30 seasons, meaning their coaches are doing something right. In fact, in the past 30 years, only two Capitals coaches have failed to guide their team to the postseason.

BRYAN MURRAY Bryan Murray coached the Capitals from 1981 to 1990. He led the Caps to the playoffs for the first time in franchise history in 1983, and was awarded the Jack Adams Award as Coach of the Year in 1984. Murray helped the Capitals advance to the postseason in seven straight seasons before being replaced by his younger brother, Terry Murray, in 1990.

RON WILSON Ron Wilson coached the Capitals for five seasons beginning in 1997, None of those seasons were more successful than his first, when the Caps reached the Stanley Cup Final for the first and only time in team history. Wilson was known as a leader and as a pioneer, using computer technology to assist with game preparation.

BARRY TROTZ In May 2014, Barry Trotz was announced as the new coach of the Capitals. Trotz took over a talented Capitals team that had qualified for the playoffs in each season from 2008 to 2013. With only four players over 30 years old, perhaps Trotz's greatest challenge will be helping his young stars learn how to be winners in the NHL.

Fans and the Internet

Slap Shot is the Capitals' mascot, which is a character that represents the team. He is a patriotic bald eagle who has been skating for the Caps since 1995.

The Capitals have a few fan traditions that are quite unique. When the Capitals score a goal, fans will routinely shout, "It's all your fault!" at the other goalie. Another tradition comes from a fan named William Stillwell, known as "Goat." It is his booming voice coming from Section 105 that leads thousands of fans in chants during home games. "The Horn Guy," also known as Sam Wolk, is another famous fan. Wolk sits in Section 415 and blows out three blasts on a horn, to which the arena responds, "Let's Go Caps!"

Japers Rink is a well-known Capitals blog and online community where fans can talk about the team. In addition, the Washington Post offers a blog known as Capitals Insider, which offers additional team and player statistics, as well as articles and interviews.

Signs
of a fan

#1 During the National Anthem, many fans can be heard shouting the "Oh" extra loudly, during the line, "Oh, say does that star-spangled banner yet wave…"

#2 The 2014–2015 Caps Kids Club offers exclusive pictures, videos, and games, as well as a Nicklas Backstrom bobblehead.

Legends of the Past

Many great players have suited up for the Caps. A few of them have become icons of the team and the city it represents.

Mike Gartner

Mike Gartner is known as one of the fastest skaters in NHL history, with an accurate shot to go along with his blazing speed. Gartner began his career in the WHA with the Cincinnati Stingers before signing with the Caps. At just 20 years old he was a runner up to Wayne Gretzky for Rookie-of-the-Year honors, leading the Caps in both goals, 36, and points, 68. Gartner was a eight-time **All-Star** and was inducted into the Hockey Hall of Fame in 2001.

Position: Right Wing
NHL Seasons: 25 (1979–1998)
Born: October 29, 1959, in Ottawa, Ontario, Canada

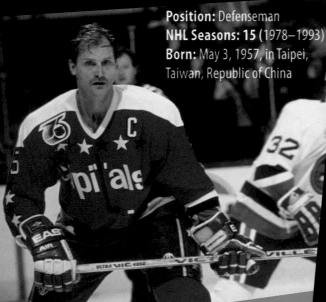

Position: Defenseman
NHL Seasons: 15 (1978–1993)
Born: May 3, 1957, in Taipei, Taiwan, Republic of China

Rod Langway

Rod Langway played 11 of his 16 seasons with the Capitals. Though he was not much of a goal scorer, he is fondly remembered for his game-winning goal against the New York Rangers during the 1990 playoffs. More significantly, Langway and his tenacious defensive play were credited with lowering the Caps' **goals against average** dramatically and helping them to become a perennial playoff team. A two-time winner of the James Norris Memorial Trophy as the top defenseman in the NHL, Langway earned the nickname, "Secretary of Defense."

Dale Hunter

Dale Hunter was a talented offensive player who played 19 seasons for Quebec, Washington, and Colorado. He is one of four Capitals to have their jerseys retired. Hunter was a team captain who played center and scored more than 1,000 points in his NHL career. His 2,003 penalty minutes remain a franchise record. Referred to often as the heart and soul of the Capitals, the talented center, upon retiring, was famously quoted as saying, "I'm not a Wayne Gretzky. I just tried to give my all every night."

Position: Center
NHL Seasons: 21 (1980–1999)
Born: July 31, 1960, in Petrolia, Ontario, Canada

Peter Bondra

Peter Bondra, who began his professional hockey career at just 18 years old, was known for his powerful and accurate slap shot. Bondra scored 50 goals in a season twice and became the 37th player in NHL history to score 500 career goals. Before being traded to the Ottawa Senators, Bondra etched his name everywhere in the Capitals' record books. As of 2014, he still holds the team's records for goals, points, game-winning goals, short-handed goals, and **hat tricks**.

Position: Right Wing
NHL Seasons: 18 (1990–2007)
Born: February 7, 1968, Lutsk, Ukrainian Soviet Socialist Republic, Soviet Union

Stars of Today

Today's Capitals team is made up of many young, talented players who have proven that they are among the best in the league.

Alexander Ovechkin

In the 2002 Under-18 World Championships, Alexander Ovechkin scored 14 goals in just eight games. Two years later, he was chosen first overall in the 2004 NHL **Entry Draft** by the Capitals. Ovechkin lived up to the great expectations immediately, scoring 106 points during his rookie season on his way to winning the Calder Memorial Trophy as Rookie of the Year. He has made the All-Star team in each of his first nine seasons, has been decorated with many prestigious awards, and has collected more than 100 points in a single season four times. In 2007–2008, Ovechkin signed a $124 million contract, the largest in the history of the NHL.

Position: Left Wing
NHL Seasons: 10 (2005–Present)
Born: September 17, 1985, in Moscow, Russia

Nicklas Backstrom

Nicklas Backstrom was a great young hockey player in his native Sweden. By the time he got to the NHL, experts were already comparing him to the great Swede, Peter Forsberg. Midway through his rookie season in 2007, Backstrom found himself playing center on the first **line** alongside Ovechkin. The two of them became a great scoring tandem, and Backstrom nearly won the Calder Memorial Trophy, finishing second following a strong second-half of the season. He scored 69 points that year. Six years later, he has surpassed 500 career points and remains a key member of the Caps' first line.

Position: Center
NHL Seasons: 8 (2007–Present)
Born: November 23, 1987, in Gavle, Sweden

Mike Green

Mike Green is a rare defenseman who is best known for his thunderous slap shot. During the 2007–2008 season, announcer Joe Beninati began calling him "Game-Over Green" for his many late, game-winning goals. The nickname stuck. Green has won four defenseman scoring titles during his nine-year career. The 2009–2010 season was perhaps his best, as he netted 19 goals and 57 **assists**. He has been named to the NHL All-Star team four times.

Position: Defenseman
NHL Seasons: 10 (2005–Present)
Born: October 12, 1985, in Calgary, Alberta, Canada

John Carlson

John Carlson is one of the most promising young players on the Capitals. He was drafted in 2008 as the 27th overall pick and has been an important addition to a developing defense. Carlson was also a member of the 2014 United States Olympic Hockey Team and was a member of the 2010 U.S. National Junior Team, where he scored the gold-medal winning goal to beat Canada, 6–5. While Carlson has played 293 games with the Caps and has scored 143 points, he is perhaps more valued for his toughness, a key factor for a young team building a defensive identity. During the 2013 season, Carlson led the team in both blocks and hits.

Position: Defenseman
NHL Seasons: 6 (2009–Present)
Born: January 10, 1990, in Natick, Massachusetts, United States

All-Time Records

19
Hat tricks
Peter Bondra leads the Capitals with 19 career hat tricks.

173
Power play goals
Alex Ovechkin has scored 173 **power play** goals. The star winger has taken almost 3,500 shots on goal.

983
Most games played
Calle Johansson holds the Capitals' team record for most games played, with 983.

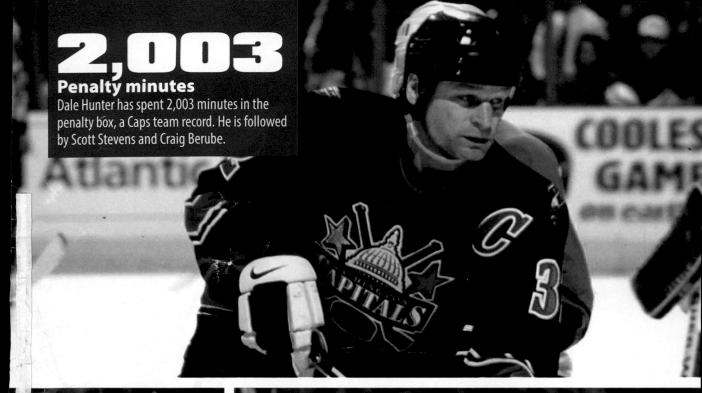

2,003
Penalty minutes
Dale Hunter has spent 2,003 minutes in the penalty box, a Caps team record. He is followed by Scott Stevens and Craig Berube.

418
Goals assisted
Michal Pivonka assisted on 418 goals, though Ovechkin is quickly closing in on his record.

Timeline

Throughout the team's history, the Washington Capitals have had many memorable events that have become defining moments for the team and its fans.

1972
The NHL grants Abe Pollin a new franchise, and Washington D.C. becomes the 17th city with an NHL hockey team, narrowly edging out San Diego and Phoenix for the honor.

1981
The Capitals achieve their first-ever double hat trick, recorded by Dennis Maruk and Tim Tookey. Each player scored three goals in a 10-4 win against the Philadelphia Flyers.

| 1973 | 1977 | 1981 | 1985 | 1989 | 1993 |

In 1975, in their second season, the Capitals finish dead last again with just 11 wins, after allowing an NHL-worst 394 goals.

1988
Dale Hunter scores an overtime goal in Game 7 of the Patrick Division Semifinal, helping the Caps to a 5-4 win. This is the first playoff series win in team history.

1983
Defenseman, Rod Langway, becomes the first American and the first Capital to win the James Norris Memorial Trophy, awarded to the top defensive player in the league.

1996

Goaltender Jim Carey is the first Washington Capitals goaltender to be awarded the Vezina Trophy as the best goaltender in the NHL that season.

The Future

The Capitals franchise waited eight full seasons before making its first trip to the playoffs. The next 30 years featured 24 playoff appearances and a trip to the Stanley Cup Final. Today, the Capitals continue to strive for their first championship behind the scoring duo of Ovechkin and Backstrom, and a young defense, gaining a reputation for speed and toughness, led by Carlson and Green.

1999

Abe Pollin sells the Capitals.

| 1997 | 2001 | | 2005 | 2009 | 2013 | 2017 |

In 2004, the Capitals are fortunate and win the NHL Entry Draft lottery for the first time since 1976. They draft the great left winger, Alexander Ovechkin, with the first overall pick in the draft.

2013

After a late-season hot streak that propelled the Caps into the playoffs, they lose to the Rangers in a deciding game 7 at the Verizon Center.

2006

Alexander Ovechkin scores "The Goal" against the Phoenix Coyotes on a play that some experts call the greatest goal of all time. Earlier in the season, Ovechkin records his first hat trick in a victory over the Anaheim Ducks.

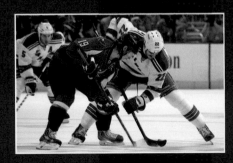

Write a Biography

Life Story

A person's life story can be the subject of a book. This kind of book is called a biography. Biographies often describe the lives of people who have achieved great success. These people may be alive today, or they may have lived many years ago. Reading a biography can help you learn more about a great person.

Get the Facts

Use this book, and research in the library and on the internet, to find out more about your favorite Cap. Learn as much about this player as you can. What position does he play? What are his statistics in important categories? Has he set any records? Also, be sure to write down key events in the person's life. What was his childhood like? What has he accomplished off the field? Is there anything else that makes this person special or unusual?

Use the Concept Web

A concept web is a useful research tool. Read the questions in the concept web on the following page. Answer the questions in your notebook. Your answers will help you write a biography.

Concept We

Adulthood
- Where does this individual currently reside?
- Does he or she have a family?

Your Opinion
- What did you learn from the books you read in your research?
- Would you suggest these books to others?
- Was anything missing from these books?

Childhood
- Where and when was this person born?
- Describe his or her parents, siblings, and friends.
- Did this person grow up in unusual circumstances?

Accomplishments off the Field
- What is this person's life's work?
- Has he or she received awards or recognition for accomplishments?
- How have this person's accomplishments served others?

Write a Biography

Help and Obstacles
- Did this individual have a positive attitude?
- Did he or she receive help from others?
- Did this person have a mentor?
- Did this person face any hardships?
- If so, how were the hardships overcome?

Accomplishments on the Field
- What records does this person hold?
- What key games and plays have defined his career?
- What are his stats in categories important to his position?

Work and Preparation
- What was this person's education?
- What was his or her work experience?
- How does this person work?
- What is the process he or she uses?

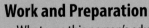

Trivia Time

Take this quiz to test your knowledge of the Capitals. The answers are printed upside down under each question.

1 What year did the Capitals franchise begin?

A. 1974

2 Who was the original owner of the Capitals?

A. Abe Pollin

3 What is the current name of the Capitals' home arena?

A. Verizon Center

4 Who is the Capitals current head coach?

A. Barry Trotz

5 How many playoff appearances have the Capitals made in team history?

A. 24

6 Which player did the Capitals choose in the 2004 NHL Entry Draft with the first overall pick?

A. Alexander Ovechkin

7 Which player was nicknamed the "Secretary of Defense"?

A. Rod Langway

8 How many coaches have the Capitals had in their 40-year history?

A. 17

9 What was Capitals player Olaf Kolzig's nickname?

A. Olie the Goalie

Key Words

All-Star: a game made for the best-ranked players in the NHL that happens mid-season. A player can be named an All-Star and then be sent to play in this game.

assists: a statistic that is attributed to up to two players of the scoring team who shoot, pass, or deflect the puck toward the scoring teammate

entry draft: an annual meeting where different teams in the NHL are allowed to pick new, young players who can join their teams

expansion: expansion in the NHL is marked by the addition of a new franchise. The league last expanded in 2000 when the Columbus Blue Jackets and Minnesota Wild joined the NHL.

franchise: a team that is a member of a professional sports league

goals against average: a statistic that is the average of goals allowed per game by a goaltender

hat tricks: when a player scores three goals in one game

line: forwards who play in a group, or "shift," during a game

playoff: a series of games that occur after regular season play

power play: when a player from one team is in the penalty box, the other team gains an advantage in the number of players

rookie: a player age 26 or younger who has played no more than 25 games in a previous season, nor six or more games in two previous seasons

World Hockey Association (WHA): the North American professional hockey league that merged with the NHL in 1979

Index

Log on to www.av2books.com

AV² by Weigl brings you media enhanced books that support active learning. Go to www.av2books.com, and enter the special code found on page 2 of this book. You will gain access to enriched and enhanced content that supplements and complements this book. Content includes video, audio, weblinks, quizzes, a slide show, and activities.

AV² Online Navigation

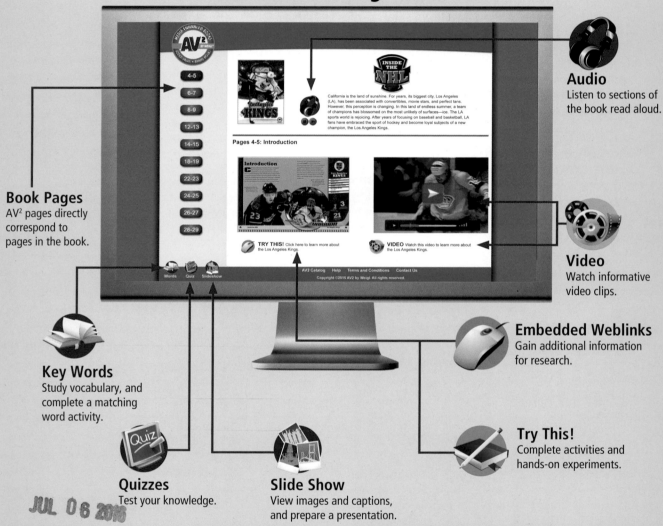

Book Pages
AV² pages directly correspond to pages in the book.

Audio
Listen to sections of the book read aloud.

Video
Watch informative video clips.

Embedded Weblinks
Gain additional information for research.

Key Words
Study vocabulary, and complete a matching word activity.

Try This!
Complete activities and hands-on experiments.

Quizzes
Test your knowledge.

Slide Show
View images and captions, and prepare a presentation.

JUL 06 2016

AV² was built to bridge the gap between print and digital. We encourage you to tell us what you like and what you want to see in the future.

Sign up to be an AV² Ambassador at www.av2books.com/ambassador.